Margin Notes

Victor Klimoski

Prior Avenue Publications
Saint Paul, Minnesota

2017

ISBN-13: 978-1540644411
ISBN-10: 1540644413

Printed in the USA by Createspace.com

Cover Design by DJ Vail

First Word Forward

The pen is patient.
Its work simple enough:
to let your hand
trace upon a page
a thought wandered in,
one that lingers and asks
a question or opens a door,
the heavy door you keep locked
so whatever lies behind it
stays well out of sight
                    and mind.

But every once in a while,
maybe at full moon or solstice,
you crack the door open,
let light and darkness flow in,
for light only knows itself
in companionship with the dark.
Their comingling tempers both,
the dark pulled into view
and light softened at the edges.
All this sets the mind to work,
the hand to serve it dutifully,
and the pen – the patient pen –
ready to help keep the record
                    straight.

*

Margin Notes

There is the story we easily tell,
the chapters neatly drawn,
the plot laid out unbroken.
It is a fine story, mostly true,
holding details we can recite
like the ingredients of a family recipe.

The other story, the one we neglect,
we keep in a grocery bag crammed
with yellowed clippings, scrawled lines,
and photographs without captions.
In the jumble another tale waits,
hasty notes written in the margins.

This is a story of imperfection,
the kind we hear and wonder
why it took so long to figure out,
or why it still holds us hostage
as though the past has a beating heart
and strength to trap us in a corner.

So we begin to tell a new story,
a story with uneven seams
and raveled edges in plain view.
We tell it first to ourselves
as we listen to its whispered voice,
        the voice that counsels courage.

Finding A Way Out

If you get lost in a maze,
its hedged walls dense and high,
you bump into dead-ends,
circle back, lose your bearings.
Panic rises, your heart beats an alarm.
You try to draw a mental map,
but it lacks a compass point.
There are no cairns, no fallen trees,
only wall after wall of leaves
that hold their heartless silence.

Then you begin by snapping a twig
or heaping a small mound of dirt
to mark a route ended in failure.
Slowly, you eliminate false starts
and feel the soft edge of calmness
as you turn this way, then that,
to see, finally, an open archway,
and beyond it the long sweep
                    of meadow.

Dark Thoughts

Dark thoughts roll in
like a prairie storm
that pushes back the light,
squeezing it into crevices,
and blocking easy escape.

Sometimes it passes quickly.
But other times, windows rattle
and shingles fly off into the night
as though the Last Judgment
was suddenly coming due.

How long a storm lasts
depends on conditions
not under our control,
though we can do more
than cower in the cellar.

For we can light a candle,
read the barometer and assess
what provisions we have
and what we might read
until it is safe to go outside,
                              again.

By Feel Alone

On a clear morning,
first light carves a crisp hard line
across the steel black sky.
A lingering cloud,
caught without an exit,
is as startled as we,
when our upended darkness
reveals the sorry seams we made
as we tried to stitch them
      by feel alone.

The Door

It is the Door,
the one we fear,
the one whose lock
shuts up like a fist,
whose knob is cold
and will not turn.
We see the Door,
pass by quickly,
afraid even a glance
might stop us dead.

But one day we do stop,
face it squarely.
We grasp the knob,
its cold biting our hand.
We pull and the Door
   swings wide,
and we never quite see
what we feared most,
just its shadow,
   dissolving,
in the rush of light.

Night Journey

In the middle of the night,
when nothing's to be done
and Worry wanders into my room,
I leave my bed and its failed sleep.
The house has taken Darkness
as its new lover, turned its back
as I move about, cautious and alert.
What once offered easy passage
has now become alien terrain.

This time of disturbance will pass.
The Earth turns toward the light,
an eager acolyte of hope.
The cycle of night and day follows
its orderly course, indifferent
to my oddly-timed wandering.
When finally I return to bed,
it has no memory of my absence
except the pillow, clenched and cold.

Shame

It has a little voice,
soft as a purring cat.
And it sits still,
like a cat,
in the mind's lap,
softly curled
under the heart.
When you move,
decide to act,
it burrows into you
looking at you
with sad eyes that ask
if, really, this is something
you should do,
can do,
given the day's burdens
and your own knack
for failure.

Unraveling

If you start to unravel
the seamless garment of your life,
if you pull at a wayward thread
thinking it a harmless gesture,
you may end up naked
for all the world to see.

But some say this is how we shed
       our fool's clothing
and the way it shields our naiveté.
This is good, we are told, for we hide
behind fabricated versions of self,
none telling the whole truth.

Unraveled, we're suddenly free.
We become again the pupil,
for what we knew for sure is less so.
In time we will step into the light,
not conscious we are naked
and overtaken by how it feels
to have the sun warm
       our bleached bodies.

Etymology of Fear

Every fear seems larger
when it prowls, nameless,
        into our nights
like a wrathful thunderhead
that booms us into submission.

Give it a name,
look into its eyes,
and, as sunlight thins the fury
        of a summer storm,
                fear finds its rightful size.

Then we can banish it
to a new landscape,
        one we have power to map,
plotting alternate routes
        as the need arises.

Knot Undone

We pick apart the mess of knots.
tracing their source one by one.
When we pull one string free,
there is another, then another,
the task endless and annoying.
We want freedom from knots
and their maleficent ways.
We want to stride forward,
not be stuck squinting at a knot
and its nagging lesson
of what haste makes.

Conversatio

Just when you are treading water,
flailing to keep your head in the air,
you feel your toes touch solid ground
and know now you will get to shore.

You emerge wet and cold,
your teeth tapping a condemnation.
But you pay no heed, only sigh,
relieved your choice did not spell doom.

Though now you face a new dilemma,
one that comes once you're warm and dry,
comes weeks later on a sunny day
when you think how nice a swim might be.

Keeping In Mind

How dark the time seemed,
hands unable to lift the load,
back bent like a street beggar.

Leaden feet could not find a stride.
What progress there was inched along
on the bruised soles of trial and error.

At last a faint light thinned the gloom,
as the road came into view,
not straight or smooth, but forward.

Too Great An Expectation

Life is complex enough already,
the path mined with jagged stones,
twisted roots, and unseen sinkholes.
Can't daily life be simple,
begun in sunshine, quiet prayer,
maybe some yoga, and then
weeding the garden or stacking wood?
Why must it require something more:
a pulsing question or an obtuse koan
perplexing me deep into the night?
Isn't it enough to get up at dawn,
see the day through to the end,
make no enemies, and sow
a few seeds of kindness?
Who said we need a mission
or need to choose this, reject that?
The big black cat next door
spends his day hunting birds.
I doubt he's thought once
            about enlightenment.

When Light Comes

These are times of great clutter,
days forested with dutiful tasks,
the undergrowth so thick
we miss the dance of light in the trees.

We wait too often in darkness
cast by our inattention.

Light transforms the ordinary,
gilds the dullest day. It shines
in the eyes of the stranger and
turns dead grass to gold.

When we finally look up,
we learn the First Truth:

It is not work that burdens us,
but thoughtless veiling of our hearts
from little clues, written daily
in the pale script of morning light.

Nineveh Is Old School

Changing our ways
does not require sackcloth,
ash-smudged heads, or placards
spelling fast-approaching doom.
It comes in the simple, whispered, *yes*,
when the fog finally lifts and we can see.
It is like the gray cat on the stoop,
knowing the door will open in due time,
poised to rush in when it does.

Learning Hard Lessons

The first time the starling hit the glass,
I thought it was bad judgment.
The second might have been scientific -
the bird's need to verify the obstacle.
By the third and fourth times,
I concluded stupidity was at work
or silly disregard for concrete fact.

What is it makes the bird repeat
again and again what is so painful?
What does the glass possess he so desires
he'd risk his tiny boned neck to get?
Beyond the glass is a barren world.
There are no trees, no berry bushes,
no small bugs clinging to stems of grass.

The bird suffers from misguided desire.
Perhaps he will go away for a few days,
avoid temptation or try to content himself
with what lies on the safe side of the glass.
And a new week may find him weighing
what he has learned about windows
and the hard lesson of not paying heed.

A Lesson On Perfection

Understanding we are all incomplete,
each in our own peculiar way,
frees us from the foolishness of perfection
and the way it cuts off our breath.

Or the way it can cast a bitter pall
even in our finest moments, when we see
all the ways it should have been better,
closer to some standard we never meet.

No one is perfect, everyone fails.
In this truth lies freedom from worry,
false worry that the crowds will gasp
when they see deep cracks in our veneer.

Not perfection, but progress is the goal,
the steady effort to strive boldly,
knowing pratfalls are part of the journey
but ready to get up and start again.

A Wandering Mind

More often now than ever before,
my mind wanders off,
   unaccompanied,
losing itself in reverie
or rehashing a bearded event
that - if it ever happened -
bears little resemblance to fact.

This streak of independence,
once thought a bit quirky,
is annoying, for it leaves me
     blankfaced,
making sense of random thoughts
strewn like shells found at dawn
on a beach smoothed and glistening.

I try to tell it of its errors,
reprimand its wandering off.
But it does not fear getting lost
or even ending up in someone
else's head - a consequence
it should not take lightly
or presume will be an improvement.

Pay Attention

Birds fly south, then north
without a book of maps.
Seasons change, seeds sprout,
and leaves know just when to fall.
Amid such simple routine, we fret
at how fate eludes prescription
and worry a wasted surcharge
for a future we cannot own.

What we have for sure
are capacities for breath and sight,
freedom to move across space,
and power to touch universes
that pulse within stone and bark
and water, each moving forward,
not knowing for certain
      what the future holds.

Stand Still

The way of peace,
the Old Master said,
is standing still:
        standing still
when the world
spins chaotically,
blazes a trail littered
with shooting stars.
Be still, he says, as you teeter
on the edge of discovery.
Let the fire of the stars
singe the tips of your hair.
Feed your doubts
great gulps of light
until you glow,
phosphorescent,
a shimmering beacon
in the gloom.

Stay Awake

In the course of a day,
you might stumble upon something
that snaps you awake,
and you suddenly see,
    with new eyes,
how things work -
    how you work -
how life's disparate parts
find their mysterious unity.
In that moment,
take up your narrative anew,
not afraid of its tragedy and doubt,
and willing no longer
    to be their blind acolyte.
Instead, follow the thread
into places you need to go,
alert to signposts and cairns
    that guide you,
if not on roads straight and smooth,
at least toward what,
    in the distance,
you recognize as light.

Gratitude

Gratitude is a kind companion
who walks quietly by your side,
pointing out what you miss
or take for granted.

Gratitude teaches you
to catch your breathe,
helps your eyes see through
the veil of petty annoyance.

Gratitude keeps pride in check
and speaks the language of humility,
knowing what comes our way
is always treasure, even if wrapped
    in plain, brown paper.

What We Do

For Susan Bourauel OSB

Like drops of rain,
what we do
fades quickly enough,
seems to disappear,
though its imprint
lasts longer than we know.
Like rain on dry soil,
what we do sinks deep,
stirs what is dormant
and drives it,
      in its time,
toward the Sun.

A New Calendar

A new year begins.
It anticipates the sum of days,
not knowing their content,
though waves of hope
wash up on undefined shores.
Seasons in an ancient pattern
come and go, each arrival
      a forgotten surprise.
How this new year will be weighed
depends on what we cannot know,
though our deeds will tip the scales,
determining where the balance lies.

Relief

Go down to the water's edge.
Stand still, spread your arms wide.
Breathe out slowly, letting go
all the worries you catalogue
for quick reference at night.
Let your eyes fill up
with the frothing blue of the water
comingled with the sky's bunting,
an estuary of color to calm your soul.
Feel the sun on your face,
swallow great gulps of light
to feed your famished heart.
Dip your hand into the water.
Let its cold quicken your blood
as it pulses through your veins,
steeling you, not against defeat,
but for all life's possibilities.

Stay Alert

What is the song of the bird
we hear deep in the forest?
How does light on water
teach the rainbow its trade?
When we enter love's presence,
why does our breath slow,
our heart beat fast?

What do we see when we peer
past the last shadows into dawn?
Why do we worry over efforts
to decipher the whole story
when we have the chapters,
each connecting to the next,
their web of clues offering us
      instruction:
          when to act,
          when to yield.

No Shortcuts

Despite our desire
for ironclad rules
or foolproof steps,
the search for happiness
    falls short
when we miss signs
found in the creased folds
    of everyday life.

Silence

If you seek peace,
still your tongues
and quell your mind's chatter,
then you are free
to ask a blessing:
a burning coal,
      red hot,
to sear your mouths
and set them free
      for song.

Not As Simple As It Seems

If you are facing in the right direction,
all you need do is keep walking – Buddha

The problem, Buddha,
as you well know,
is where to face.
Too quickly done
leads to misadventure.
Thoughtlessly begun
ends up in blind alleys,
like so many plans
where a best guess
        is no guess at all.

So it comes down to choice,
deciding where it is
you want to end up,
then turning,
planting your feet squarely,
alert to your surroundings,
and leaving small clues
        along the path
to find your way back –
        just in case.

Creeds and Questions

If images of God were solidly one,
if what constitutes the faithful way
was scribed the same on every heart,
then perhaps a creed could speak
in one voice with one, singular tone.

But humans seldom fall in line
even when they march in unison.
Notions of God filter through
human stories, their dialects marked
more by question than by fact.

Some find their way to wise masters,
some to the latest dime store preacher.
But even then, with ideas fat or thin,
no sure conclusion plots a straight path,
one free of blind turns and potholes.

Instead, we learn to retell the story
as we wrestle with life's daily lessons,
the way they teach us to see anew,
to let go our need for steeled answers,
to rest content in the cloud of seeking.

This story will draw us nearer to truth,
truth exceeding the reach of fact,
revealing itself in a voice
we can no longer dismiss as alien
but unavoidably the echo of our own.

Feast of Poor Souls

We often spoke of them as poor,
the ill-equipped for heaven,
pages missing from their visas.
By their fault or benign neglect,
they fell short of the standard,
were sent to work off the blot
in a land of gray afternoons
and long, dark, cold nights.

Using arrogant human measures,
we imagined this in-between space,
unschooled in the capacity of God
to assess the worth of a soul
while weighing a lifetime of hazards.
Our calibrations, exact and clear,
never rounded up or allowed a gap.
The fit must be perfect or not at all.

But our poverty of perspective
confuses mercy with a commodity,
treats it like a scale of brass precision.
Mercy flows like a river in spring,
spilling extravagantly over the banks.
It moves like the wind, gathering
and carrying each soul home,
a place of light where welcome
         replaces exile.

Cemetery At Abbey Dore, Herefordshire

Hallowed is this ground
by custom and ritual,
the last place they were known,
their names carved on stones
thought to last forever.
But like our bodies, these markers,
bearing the simplest details,
yield to the persistent tides
      of time and decay.

Today we know only that John died,
aged fifty-something, the date obscured.
And here lies a widow (maybe Hannah?)
who outlived her husband – illegible –
      her age lost forever.
Broken markers scatter others,
their names carried off by weeds.

This plot of land in its disarray
teaches curious visitors like us
that what seems invincible
in the end returns to the earth,
that even chiseled stone is no match
for the slow but steady erosion
of wind and season and time.

Paying Respects

Cemetery, Langlade, Wisconsin

Heavy dew weighs down the grass,
but still it sighs under each step.
The angle of the Sun masks
the headstones but not their truth.

Norway pine that once sheltered my people
have been cut down, altering the landscape -
though nothing changes the permanence
of where my people lie, quiet and still.

Everything else is changing.
People grow old and die,
and this field of grief receives them
where thoughts of immortality vanish.

When someone comes and reads the names,
do they feel a chill, a premonition,
then turn quickly to retrace their steps,
lest they forget where the exit lies?

Or do they sigh, recognizing
a graced pattern written in histories
reaching backward and forward, continuing
to tell a story dazzling in its mystery
                    and tempering fear?

Growing Old

In Memory of Patricia Klimoski Lambert

My sister sits on a white folding chair,
staring out at the dance hall floor.
As couples swirl and spin,
she sips coffee from an empty cup.
She loses the names of old neighbors,
though not details of stories they shared.
Neither unhappy or overly afraid,
she spends courage she's banked for years,
wonders when she drops a name
or puts scissors in the freezer,
whether this just comes with age
or is how a soul begins its journey

                      home.

Mickey Krile At Prayer
A Memorial Poem

You see her, framed in the window, as she looks at the storm raging like a mad bull. She protested every time, saying the younger men could tend the lines. And every time he consoled her knowing she would ignore his reassurance. It was what they learned to do: one going out into the night, the other keeping watch. As he prepared, she said her first prayer.

She prayed as she ran water for coffee, and she prayed as she poured them each a cup, strong and black. He kissed her at the door, and as she closed the door, she prayed again, wondering if she had said enough to him. Then she stood at the window, watching him drive away, the silence of the house wrapping its arms around her.

She kept her vigil in the kitchen, sitting at the table with her prayer book, the *Herald*, and a pack of Pall Malls. The prayers, said hundreds of times before, spoke a familiar comfort. She re-read the news to sharpen her opinions and distract her from the storm that forced its way upon her.

As the hours passed, she smoked and read, pausing to pray as she glanced at the window now fringed with light. When finally she heard his truck, the way the door called out its high-pitched greeting, she got up and watched him step into the wind. He saw her, smiled and waved. And she would wave, her fingers lightly touching her lips. As she walked to the door, she said one more prayer, not the last one, but the one she liked the best.

The Wren

In Memory of Laura Murphy

Her aged heart is struggling,
a wren flying into a fierce wind
with hopes of landing safely.
She has no fear of dying,
a lesson long life can teach,
though she's unsure of the passage,
where everything is the first time.
Her breath rises and falls slowly,
a fluttering sound like a bird
landing on a sturdy branch,
finding refuge at last
as the night folds itself around her.

A Final Testament

A Memorial For My Father

We always underestimated you,
thinking you uncomplicated.
None of us ever asked
what you dreamed to be,
if your lot was your choosing
or what you thought beautiful.
We could index your faults,
passed our judgment on them,
harsh and quite sure we'd never
let ourselves fall so short,
> be found so wanting.

But now when we tell our stories,
we recall your generosity,
your kindness towards strangers,
the remorse when you failed,
a piety you kept from public view.
What we don't know fills pages,
but what we recount are these virtues,
winnowed from a complex life,
the only things,
> now,
> that matter.

Loss of Ordinary Time
In Memory of Mary Ann Callahan

We counte time by her absence,
the days since she died,
months without her voice
giving advice or making us laugh.
This calendar of memory defined
our grief, the deep fracture
in what we once called ordinary life.

In a while, balance returned.
Friday was now just Friday
and not the day she died.
Time passed without much notice,
usual work done, routine restored.
But every so often, without warning,
her absence overwhelms us,
and we know, in our bones,
how time is anything
              but ordinary.

The Best Lesson

In Memory of Jack Huntley

The best lesson he taught us
was not how to die bravely,
but how to live attentively.
Each day came with no assumptions,
except its gift, opening at first light
and moving quietly through his gardens.
If fireworks sould suddenly explode,
he would delight in the extravagance.
If not, he would still smile,
for this day,

      the one before him,

was all he needed -
the pulse of the Earth,
the power of the Sun,
the soft touch of love.

Epiphany Morning

In Memory of Fr. Charles Froehle

If there could be a right day,
a day rich with holy sign,
it is this day of star power.
Its ancient promise
shocked the world awake
as it did him early on,
lit a way he followed,
steady and true.

It is right, then, that his life,
eked out these past months,
should pass into a star-bright sky.
Everything he believed -
the song of his soul -
has come to meet him,
to take his hand and stand
him in the golden beams
spilling over the dark horizon.
All sadness gone,
     all sorrow fled,
he has opened his great arms,
unbound and free.

Abundance

Mercy flows in a wide path.
It crosses every life, seeping
into the pores of the frantic –
as generous with the least
as it is with the noble,
the foolish as with the wise.

Mercy is an unplumbed pool,
rises from depthless abundance
and frees the heart of its burdens.
To those who might turn away, afraid,
it returns again and again. Mercy
is a well from which we draw
without fear of coming up dry.

Interpretation

They are ours, these refugees,
their names obliterated,
their bodies torn, their souls
bruised and nearly broken.
It matters, the mindless slaughter
in Charleston, in Sandy Hook,
in the daily streets of Chicago.
It is not old news, events in Belgium
and Paris, in Syria's dark,
      unceasing nightmare.

Like streams rushing to the sea,
our fate is bound with all these.
We are not excused,
untouched by the messy communion
that comes as birthright,
      that comes as duty.

Leave Them Nameless

Leave the poor unnamed.
Let them scavenge what's left
after we've had our fill,
the scraps a fine meal
given their lack of effort.

Name them and they might
presume our charity
is more than it is.
"Poor" is fit title,
saying all that's true.

Names confuse the roles
we've set for us both -
we who merit our lot
and they who reap
what failed effort sows.

Speechless

My immigrant father lost his voice
when words he knew by heart
provoked smirking neighbors
who mocked the sounds he made.

When he finally found a voice like theirs,
no longer the butt of their scorn,
he vowed in his child's heart
he would never be shamed again.
So words formed in his infant's mind
collapsed into a pile of dust,
swept away by a sour gust of wind
he now knew by one name only.

The Politics of Anger

Anger feeds on despair,
the thin gruel of regret,
when everything seems bleak,
affliction beyond human cure.

Anger boils the mind dry,
fired with scraps of rumor,
half-truths, amused deceit,
tinder for an endless lie.

Anger binds throats with twine,
speech pulling the knot tight.
In time the only sounds are
rasped curses, high-pitched whines.

Anger shreds a crowd into tiny bits,
flesh and spit slicking the streets.
Darkness descends, hearts turn to stone,
and people's souls left for dead.

Ayn Rand Comments on the Bible

The way they tell it,
no one's left behind,
everyone counts,
even those who wander off
or have a bad leg
or show up late in the day.
Such a homely tale falls short.
The idea all are deserving
weighs down progress,
foiled by those who fall behind
no matter the incentives.
Stories about "common good"
allow for no distinctions, punish
the few who long ago learned
that it's every man for himself.

Aging: A Meditation

It is a brazen affront, this aging thing,
this relentless drive to a far distant horizon
where light fades and the unknown begins.

Nothing's to be done to slow its progress,
its daily erosions and frequent taunts
aimed at one's defiant resistance.

The world coins softer, coddled, words
meant to lessen the blow, offer comfort
against the hard landing of the truth.

The softest words lack the density of fact:
Age is a master who never blinks,
who has its way no matter what.

So I begrudge this common fate of mine,
act as though it's caught me,
if not by trickery, then by surprise.

I am left to rethink a half-made plan,
to actually wake up and pay heed
that any future always has time
                        at its back.

Calculation

What time we have
is less than we assume
when we think forever
is our right and due.
What changes our mind -
like our own Damascus storm -
catches us off guard.
What happens next
depends on the courage
to live alert and present
to this hour,
        this fate,
    this moment,
when every sense tingles
with the electric jolt
        of time.

Time in the Balance ✸

Wasted time is a moral fault
inducing guilt and recrimination.
Not so, a *waste of time,*
a judgment rendered on events
lacking a credible purpose.
Lack of time is a lament,
the keen of those with calendars
whose long tentacles bind them
in unbreakable cocoons.
Loss of time is victim of interruptions
and their nasty lack of discipline.
Lots of time is a rare commodity
quickly spent down once the owner
discovers the sudden bounty.
Time out is a form of discipline.
Time left is grudging reality
made worse by *wasted time*
              (a moral fault).
Poor timing can be bad luck
or a case of inattention,
just as *good timing* can be seen
as the gift of foresight.
Time management is a pain
except for those for whom it works.
Time to kill is a luxury.
Time away is a vacation.
Running out of time stirs panic

and the sharp realization
that all time is the price paid
for passing through life,
leaving skid marks
and not stopping at the lights.

On Not Choosing Joy

Should anyone ask,
I hate this shaft of stainless steel
driven mercilessly into my femur.
I resent the way I wobble
across a room, wondering
if the foreign joint will pop,
leaving me dangling a useless leg.
I worry over one more flawed part
and its taunt that I'm losing ground
and the illusion of besting death.
Most of all, I feel sorry for myself,
having to live with limits,
to deal with pain, and needing help
even to tie my goddam shoe.

The Pilgrim's Collage

Scraps of pictures litter the table,
images for a pilgrim to sift,
letting the heart read
what this scrap or that
tells about the soul's journey.

Slowly, a pilgrim creates a canvas,
moving pieces about carefully
until a vision appears, emerges
as a doe might emerge from the fog,
a ghostly shape growing slowly familiar.

What a pilgrim recognizes at last,
as the canvas details the journey,
is a soul's quiet narration,
what was heard along the way,
the whispered voice, too long neglected,
        freed, now, to speak aloud.

Beauty

Beauty is the charged air
after a storm,
the forest smell
on a hot afternoon.
It is the dance of clouds
across a field,
the movement rippling
like a pond shattered
      by a cast stone.
Beauty is a glass of cool water
on a summer day,
      we taste,
    then sigh,
as though we've found elixir
for the soul's deep longing.

Summer Solstice Light

Light overwhelms the world,
pours in during the small hours
and lingers late into the night.
Today, Earth falls headlong
into the embrace of the Sun
and drinks greedily of its light,
so deeply it would surely burst
if it were not for the chaste discipline
of drinking only enough
to keep it buoyant and filled
                with desire.

Holy Communion

On any summer afternoon,
I would crest the hill,
look down on the clutch of buildings
and know without a doubt -
no matter the time of day
or day of the week -
my place at table was set.

She would meet me at the door
as though she had been waiting,
as though my coming
was the highlight of her day.
She would welcome me to my place,
my place at the table by the window
where we could look out on the field
winding through the hills
like a green, feathery stream.

Soon he would come in from the barn,
shout his greeting from the back porch.
He'd walk into the kitchen,
grab my hand, patting my back
as though I were a son absent too long.
Then we would sit around the table
as they asked after my life,
each common detail received
as though a bit of wonder.

Now from the crest of the hill,
the road ends at an open field
like it's forgotten why it came.
Corn grows where the pump house stood,
and stones picked and piled
mound up where the kitchen once was,
with its table by the window,
my favorite blue cup filled with coffee,
my place always ready.

Pentecost

Feeling cold and abandoned,
they huddled behind locked doors.
Winds howled, walls shook,
the clamor deafening.
They quaked, awaiting
what surely was the end.

Stillness fell upon them,
a deep silence held
      in each heartbeat.
They felt themselves pulled
through the knothole of doubt
and then filled with warmth,
until each one glowed
as bright as the flames flaring
over their heads.

Finally, they began to speak,
their voices pitched and exotic,
for what drove them into the streets
demanded new vocabulary.

Clear Sighted

Children, once taught to pray,
pray for everything - a bush, a bell,
a granny dead before they were born.
They set no conditions nor ponder
whether a sick cat or lost ball
merits divine intervention.
They take as true the instruction
and share its bounty as though
      absolute
        fact.

Photographs

Photos are guardians
of what otherwise might be lost.
When we come across them -
a marker in a book
or wedged in the corner of a drawer -
time halts, and we can smell
the rain that had just stopped
and hear mother's voice
telling us to stand up straight.
We feel the sun in our faces
and our eyes squinted nearly shut.
We hold our breaths, squirm
      and wait for the click.
Then we move on, forgetting
everything that just happened
until the photograph calls it
          back to life.

Departure

Leaving begins long before
the door closes and the phone
rings with no one to answer.

But the day comes when you know
you no longer fit.
You speak past each other
even as you gather
around the kitchen table.

So you drift for a while,
mull your disappointment,
the loss of belonging.

In time you eat with strangers,
receive their kind greetings,
even though it's not the same.
their stories with meanings
       you just don't get.

The Cherry Tree Teaches

The cherry trees outside the window
did not spend the night in worry,
wondering if they were cherry-enough
or if their fruit was too scarce, too lush,
too red, too thinly spread along the branch,
or if they would last the change in season.

They stand, six in a row, with no regrets,
no self-conscious shyness at falling short.
They are triumphant in their cherry-ness,
sway in the morning breeze, confident,
for they know they are living their destiny
with no need to rewrite or wish it away.

Humans wonder over their lot in life,
second-guess themselves, fret and worry.
They bend toward scarcity, the fear
everyone will discover how empty their cellars,
how frayed their cuffs, how they are not enough.
They resign themselves to discontent, fail
to see how the cherry tree sways – and learn.

has made
it's peace

A Hard Fact

for Kathy, forty-two years later

A stone can be a paperweight,
            prop open a door
      block a path
               or fashion a wall.
Its atoms, packed tight,
keep out rain,
            snow,
               and bugs.

To the average eye,
it may lack beauty:
weight and heft its only claims.
Beached and washed by waves,
it takes on a sheen
until sun and air return
its dull,
            unremarkable
               coat.

But some stones catch the eye,
find their way into a tumbler
with a handful of sand
and patience to bear the noise.
After a time they change,
burnished in unimagined ways.
It doesn't happen overnight.
Sometimes it takes forty years
               - or more.

Worrying About the Wrong Thing

The masters tell us
to curb the vagabond mind,
its endless wandering, searching
for charms to undo the done
or give secret passage to a golden land.
Instead, they say, look around,
Read the text of daily life.
Don't skip over what seems plain
or rush to the first conclusion.
What is it, in this very moment,
that might let light come pouring in,
casting out gloom, freeing
you for the song or poem
you've started and never finished?

middle
of the
night

Life Lessons

Read the text of your life,
all the chapters, even those
you would prefer to skim,
if not ignore completely.

Read slowly and pause often.
Attend to details: the incidental,
random, one-time events,
things that make you wince.

Read, curious to find the thread
leading to and from secrets
and their capacity to explain
how odd parts create a whole.

Read your life as a sacred scroll
on which is writ a sacred story,
a story for your instruction and hope,
with footnotes to a grand mystery.

*

ACKNOWLEDGMENTS

Writing is often a lonely practice. Having the benefit of two critical readers who are talented writers themselves made the development and refinement of this collection much less burdensome. Ann Glumac and Kathleen Flanagan Zannoni each helped me see my poems with fresh eyes. I am very grateful for the time and attention they gave each poem.

Several poems in this collection received recognition in the 2016 annual poetry contest of the League of Minnesota Poets: "Shame" (second place, Grand View Award), "Stay Awake" (third place, Southeastern Minnesota Poets Award), "Speechless" (honorable mention, John and Helen Pappas Memorial Award) and "Margin Notes" (Lost in Translation Award).

Made in the USA
Charleston, SC
21 January 2017